SILVER CITY

CITY

publications

Project Management Professional (PMP)®

Quick Reference Guide

Michelle N. Halsey, PMP

PMP® Certification Course
Quick Reference Study Guide

ISBN-10: 1-64004-202-4

ISBN-13: 978-1-64004-202-5

©2016 Silver City Publications & Training, L.L.C.

Authored by: Michelle N. Halsey, PMP

Silver City Publications & Training, L.L.C.
P.O. Box 1914
Nampa, ID 83653

PMP is a registered mark of the Project Management Institute, Inc.

Table of Contents

Process Map 7

Organization Types 9

Triple and Expanded Constraints 10

Project Selection Methods 11

    Benefit-Cost Ratio (BCR) 11

    Economic Value Add (EVA) 11

    Internal Rate of Return (IRR) (a.k.a. discount rate) 11

    Present Value (PV) 11

    Net Present Value (NPV) 12

    Return on Investment (ROI) 12

    Return on Invested Capital (ROIC) 12

    Return on Sales (ROS) 12

    Return on Assets (ROA) 13

    Working Capital 13

    Payback Period 13

    Straight-Line Depreciation 13

    Declining Balance Depreciation 13

    Opportunity Cost 14

    Project Measurement Method Summary 14

Formulas 15

    Communication Channel Formula 15

    Normal Distribution Formulas (a.k.a. Gaussian Distribution) 16

    Beta Distribution 16

        Beta Distribution: Three-Point Estimate (Mean or Weighted Average) 16

        Beta Distribution: Standard Deviation 16

        Beta Distribution: Variance 17

    Triangular Distribution 17

        Triangular Distribution: Three-Point Estimate (Mean or Weighted Average) 17

Triangular Distribution: Standard Deviation 17

Triangular Distribution: Variance 17

7 Basic Tools of Quality 18

Cause & Effect Diagram (a.k.a. Fishbone or Ishikawa Diagram) 18

Flow Chart 18

Checklist or Check Sheet 19

Histogram 20

Scatter Diagram 20

Control Chart (a type of run chart) 21

Quality Theories 22

Earned Value Formulas 23

Network Diagram Mapping 26

Day 0 Start – AoN Formula Map 26

Day 1 Start – (AoN) Formula Map (most common) 26

Network Diagram Types 27

Activity on Node 27

Activity on Arrow 27

Schedule Compression Impact 28

Gantt Chart / PDM Relationships 28

Finish-to-Start (FS) Relationship 28

Finish-to-Finish (FF) Relationship 28

Start-to-Start (SS) Relationship 29

Start-to-Finish (SF) Relationship 29

Sample Gantt Chart 29

Risk Calculations 30

Risk Formulas 30

Decision Tree 30

Expected Monetary Value 30

Risk Response Strategies 31

Probability Basics 31

Contract Types 32

    Contract Formulas 33

    Cost Plus Fixed Fee 34

    Cost Plus Incentive Fee.. 34

    Firm Fixed Fee 35

    Fixed Price Incentive Fee 35

    Fixed Price 36

    Point of Total Assumption... 36

Stakeholder Classification Models 37

Stakeholder Engagement Assessment Matrix 37

Organizational Theories 38

Stages of Team Formation.. 39

Forms of Power... 40

Conflict Resolution Techniques 41

    Sources of Conflict 41

Basic Communication Model... 42

Group Creativity Techniques... 43

Group Decision Making Techniques 43

Ethical Decision Making Framework 44

Inputs, Tools & Techniques, and Outputs... 45

    Project Integration Management Knowledge Area.. 45

    Project Scope Management Knowledge Area 47

    Project Time Management Knowledge Area... 49

    Project Cost Management Knowledge Area 52

    Project Quality Management Knowledge Area.. 53

    Project Human Resource Management Knowledge Area.. 55

    Project Communications Management Knowledge Area... 56

    Project Risk Management Knowledge Area.. 57

Project Procurement Management Knowledge Area 60

Project Stakeholder Management Knowledge Area 61

Process Map

Knowledge Area	Project Management Process Groups				
	Initiating Process Group	Planning Process Group	Executing Process Group	Monitoring and Controlling Process Group	Closing Process Group
Project Integration Management	Develop Project Charter	Develop Project Management Plan	Direct and Manage Project Work	Monitor and Control Project Work Perform Integrated Change Control	Close Project or Phase
Project Scope Management		Plan Scope Management Collect Requirements Define Scope Create WBS		Validate Scope Control Scope	
Project Time Management		Plan Schedule Management Define Activities Sequence Activities Estimate Activity Resources Estimate Activity Durations Develop Schedule		Control Schedule	
Project Cost Management		Plan Cost Management Estimate Costs Determine Budget		Control Costs	
Project Quality Management		Plan Quality Management	Perform Quality Assurance	Control Quality	

Knowledge Area	Initiating Process Group	Planning Process Group	Executing Process Group	Monitoring and Controlling Process Group	Closing Process Group
Project Human Resource Management		Plan Human Resource Management	Acquire Project Team Develop Project Team Manage Project Team		
Project Communications Management		Plan Communications Management	Manage Communications	Control Communications	
Project Risk Management		Plan Risk Management Identify Risks Perform Qualitative Risk Management Perform Quantitative Management Plan Risk Responses		Control Risks	
Project Procurement Management		Plan Procurement Management	Conduct Procurements	Control Procurements	Close Procurements
Project Stakeholder Management	Identify Stakeholders	Plan Stakeholder Management	Manage Stakeholder Engagement	Control Stakeholder Engagement	

Organization Types

PMI Assumption: Mature organization, balanced matrix, and has a PMO unless otherwise stated

5 Organization Types
PM versus FM Level of Power

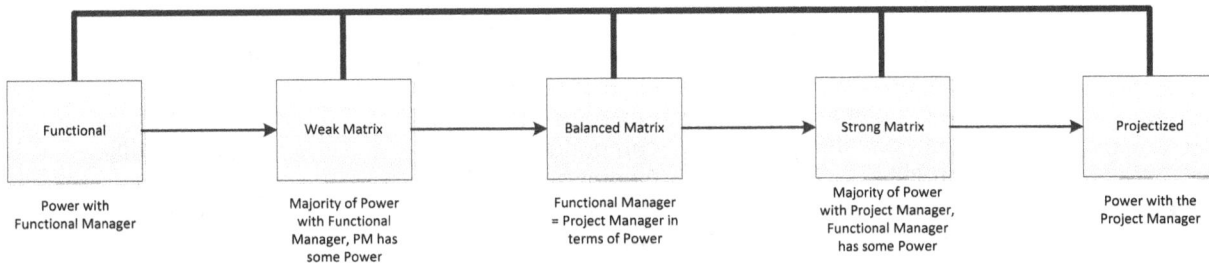

Functional	Weak Matrix	Balanced Matrix	Strong Matrix	Projectized
Power with Functional Manager	Majority of Power with Functional Manager, PM has some Power	Functional Manager = Project Manager in terms of Power	Majority of Power with Project Manager, Functional Manager has some Power	Power with the Project Manager

As you move along the continuum from left to right, the Project Manager starts with no power and gradually moves to a stronger position in the organization type

Project Characteristics	Functional	Weak Matrix	Balanced Matrix	Strong Matrix	Projectized
PM Authority	Little or None	Low	Low to Moderate Equivalent to Functional Manager	Moderate to High	High to Total
Resource Availability	Little or None	Low	Low to Moderate	Moderate to High	High to Total
Project Budget Management	Functional Manager	Functional Manager	Mixed	Project Manager	Project Manager
PM Role	Part-time Project Expeditor	Part-time Project Coordinator	Full-time Project Manager	Full-time Project Manager	Full-time Project Manager
PM Admin Staff	Part-time	Part-time	Part-time	Full-time	Full-time

Table 1 - Project, Program, and Portfolio Comparison

Domain	Projects	Programs	Portfolios
Scope	• Defined Objectives • Progressively elaborated	• Larger scope • Provide Significant Benefits	• Organizational scope • Changes with organizational strategic objectives
Change	• Expect Change • Prevent uncontrolled change	• Expect change inside/outside program • Manage change	• Continuously monitor change in internal & external environment
Planning	• Progressive elaboration of detailed plans throughout life cycle of project	• Develop program plan • High-level plans developed to guide component level planning	• Create & maintain processes & communication for aggregate portfolio
Management	• PM manages team to meet project objectives	• PrM manage program staff and PM's • Vision and leadership	• PoM manage or coordinate staff at all 3 levels • Report into aggregate portfolio
Success	• Measure by product/project quality, timeliness, budge, and customer satisfaction	• Measured by degree to which program satisfies needs & benefits	• Measured in terms of aggregate investment • Looks at performance & benefit realization
Monitoring	• Work produced (product, service, result)	• Progress of program goals to ensure overall benefit realization	• Strategic changes and aggregate results and risks

Triple and Expanded Constraints

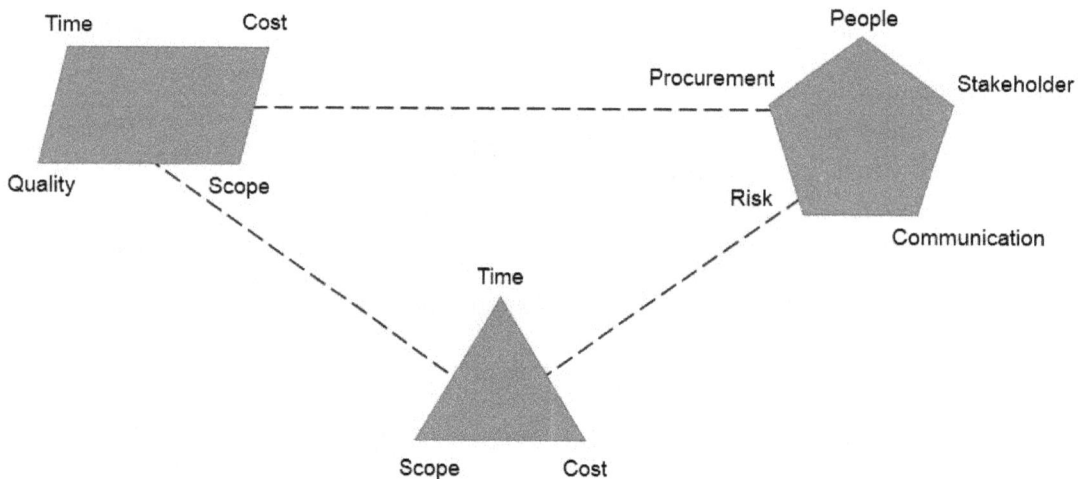

Project Selection Methods

Benefit-Cost Ratio (BCR)

The benefit cost ratio looks at the ratio of benefits to costs. It compares the present value of benefits to the present value of costs. A BCR greater than 1 means, the benefits are greater than the costs. The formula for the benefit cost ratio is:

$$BCR = \frac{Benefit}{Cost}$$

Economic Value Add (EVA)

The economic value add looks at how much value the project creates for shareholders. It looks at net profits and opportunity costs to determine if the project truly adds economic value to the organization. The EVA formula is:

$$EVA = After\ tax\ profit - (capital\ expenditures * cost\ of\ capital)$$

Internal Rate of Return (IRR) (a.k.a. discount rate)

Expresses the project returns as an interest rate. It looks at net profits and opportunity costs to determine if the project truly adds economic value to the organization. The net present value is used to identify the discounted rate, which is the internal rate of return. Generally referred to as a percentage. The higher the percentage, the greater the return, and the more desirable the project.

Present Value (PV)

The present value is based on the concept of the "time value of money" economic theory that says a dollar today is worth more than a dollar a year from now. PV takes time out of the equation so you can evaluate the value of a project. The farther out the timing of the future cash flow, the lower is the present value. The formula for PV is:

$$PV = \frac{FV}{(1+r)^n}$$

Where,

FV = future value

r = interest rate or rate of return

n = time period

Net Present Value (NPV)

The net present value is the similar to present value, except you factor in the cost of the project. The NPV uses the discounted sum of all cash flows received from the project in the calculation. The formula for NPV is:

$$-C_0 \sum_{i=1}^{T} \frac{C_i}{(1+r)^i}$$

Where

-C_0 = initial investment

C = cash flow

r = discount rate or interest rate

T = time period

Return on Investment (ROI)

The return on investment is a percentage that shows the return made by investing in something. The formula for ROI is:

$$ROI = \frac{(Benefit - Cost)}{Cost}$$

Return on Invested Capital (ROIC)

The return on invested capital measures how an organization uses money it invests in a project. It asks the question for every dollar invested, what is earned? The formula for ROIC is:

$$ROIC = \frac{Net\ Income\ After\ Tax}{Total\ Capital\ Invested}$$

Return on Sales (ROS)

Return on sales is a ratio for evaluating the operating efficiency of an organization or a project. It is sometimes referred to operating profit margin and tells you how much effectively profits are generated from revenue.

$$ROS = \frac{Net\ Income\ Before\ or\ After\ Taxes}{Total\ Sales}\ X\ 100\%$$

Return on Assets (ROA)

Return on Assets is an indicator of how profitable a company is relative to total assets. It provides information on how effectively the company can generate income from its' assets.

$$ROA = \frac{Net\ Income\ Before\ or\ After\ Taxes}{Total\ Investment} \ X\ 100\%$$

Working Capital

Working capital is the amount of money or capital the company has for special projects and day to day operations.

$$Working\ Capital = Current\ Assets - Current\ Liabilities$$

Payback Period

The payback period is how long it will take recoup an investment in a project. Payback period looks at the number of time periods it takes to recover your initial investment before profits start accumulating. When using payback period as a project selection method, smaller is better.

Straight-Line Depreciation

Straight line depreciation is a method for computing depreciation using the value of the asset evaluated against the number of years the asset is expected to be used.

$$SL\ Depreciation = \frac{Asset\ Value}{Life\ of\ Asset}$$

Declining Balance Depreciation

Declining balance depreciation is a method of depreciation for an asset that applies the depreciation rate against the non-depreciated balance.

$$Decling\ Balance\ Depreciation = \frac{Current\ Asset\ Value}{Estimated\ Total\ Life}$$

Where

Current asset value = Original Asset Value - Previous Depreciation

Opportunity Cost

The opportunity cost is the cost related to the next best available choice when choosing from mutually exclusive choices. Essentially it is the benefit you are giving up by choosing one project over another.

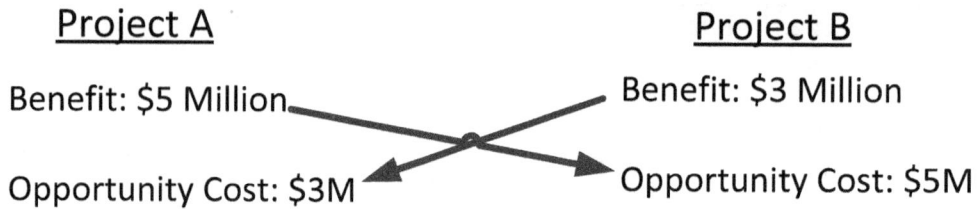

<u>Project A</u>   <u>Project B</u>

Benefit: $5 Million   Benefit: $3 Million

Opportunity Cost: $3M   Opportunity Cost: $5M

Selecting Project A rather than Project B, loses the benefit of performing Project B, therefore the opportunity cost for Project A would be $3 million in benefit for not performing Project B. This assumes the projects are mutually exclusive and only one project could be selected at the time.

Project Measurement Method Summary

Benefit Measurement Method (Bigger is Better)	Benefit Measurement Method (Smaller is Better)	Constrained Optimization Method
• **Benefit Cost Ratio (BCR)** • **Economic Value Add (EVA)** • **Internal Rate of Return (IRR)** • **Present Value (PV) or Net Present Value (NPV)** • **Return on Investment (ROI)** • **Return on Invested Capital (ROIC)**	• Opportunity Cost • Payback Period	• Linear Programming

Formulas

Communication Channel Formula

$$Communication\ Channels = \frac{n*(n-1)}{2}$$

Where n is the number of people on the team.

Note: Review the question to determine if the project manager needs to be added into the number.

Question may be asked in a variety of ways. The question may look for the number of communication channels, the change in communication channels, and the new number of communication channels.

Example:

If you have a team of 4 people, how many communication channels are there. If we draw out the lines, this would give us a diagram like the following:

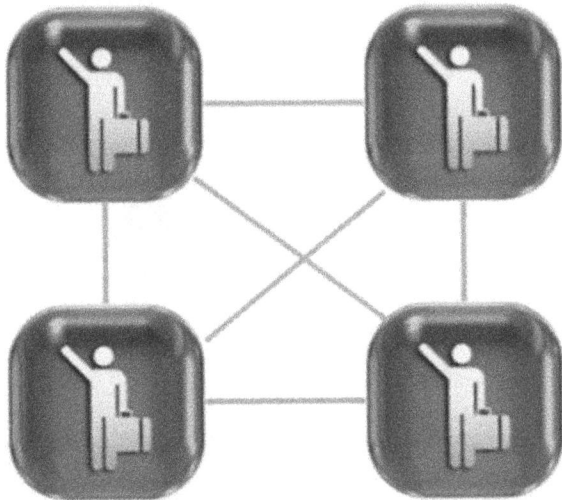

In this case, the team is small enough we could count the channels and derive 6 possible communication channels.

Using the formula, we would get the following:

$$Communication\ Channels = \frac{4*(4-1)}{2} = \frac{12}{2} = 6\ communication\ channels$$

The communication channels formula can be used to calculate the number of communication channels for large and small teams and give the project manager an idea of the complexity of communications on the project.

Normal Distribution Formulas (a.k.a. Gaussian Distribution)

Questions related to the normal distribution curve may be used in multiple knowledge areas including the Time, Cost, and Quality knowledge areas.

Six Sigma Percentages to Know

- 1 sigma = 68.27%
- 2 sigma = 95.45%
- 3 sigma = 99.73%
- 6 sigma = 99.99966%

Beta Distribution

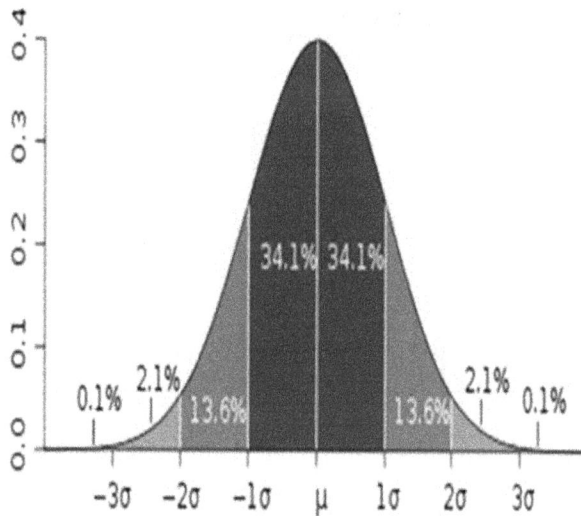

Figure 1 - Normal (Beta) Distribution Curve

Beta Distribution: Three-Point Estimate (Mean or Weighted Average)

Questions may ask for the weighted average, three-point, or PERT estimate.

$$\frac{Optimistic + 4 * Most\ Likely + Pessimistic}{6}$$

Beta Distribution: Standard Deviation

Questions may ask for the range for a value.

$$\sigma = \frac{Pessimistic - Optimistic}{6}$$

Beta Distribution: Variance

Variance = σ^2

Where σ is the standard deviation

Triangular Distribution

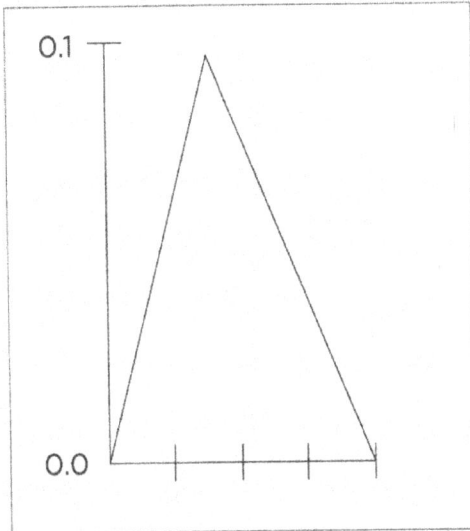

Figure 2 - Triangular Distribution

Triangular Distribution: Three-Point Estimate (Mean or Weighted Average)

Questions may ask for the weighted average, three-point, or PERT estimate.

$$\frac{Optimistic + 4 * Most\ Likely + Pessimistic}{3}$$

Triangular Distribution: Standard Deviation

Questions may ask for the range for a value.

$$\sigma = \frac{Pessimistic - Optimistic}{3}$$

Triangular Distribution: Variance

Variance = σ^2

Where σ is the standard deviation

7 Basic Tools of Quality

Cause & Effect Diagram (a.k.a. Fishbone or Ishikawa Diagram)

Purpose: Identify root cause of an issue.

Factors contributing to defect XXX

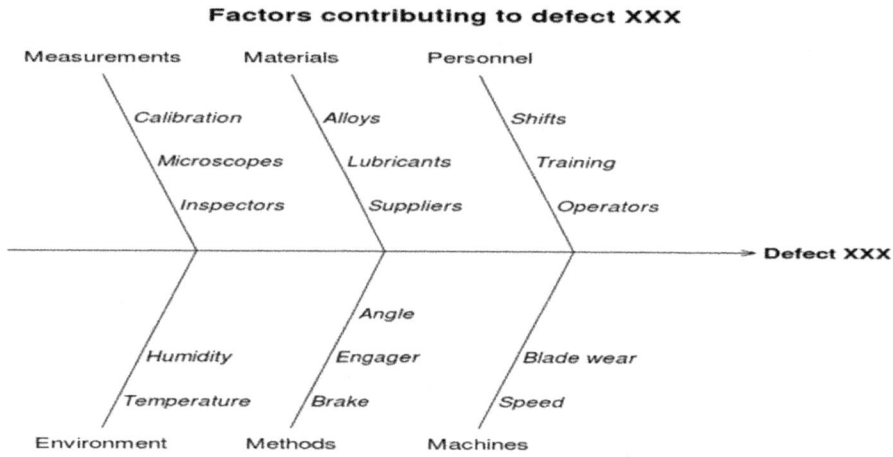

Flow Chart

Purpose: Process focused, designed to find gaps, bottlenecks, and redundancies.

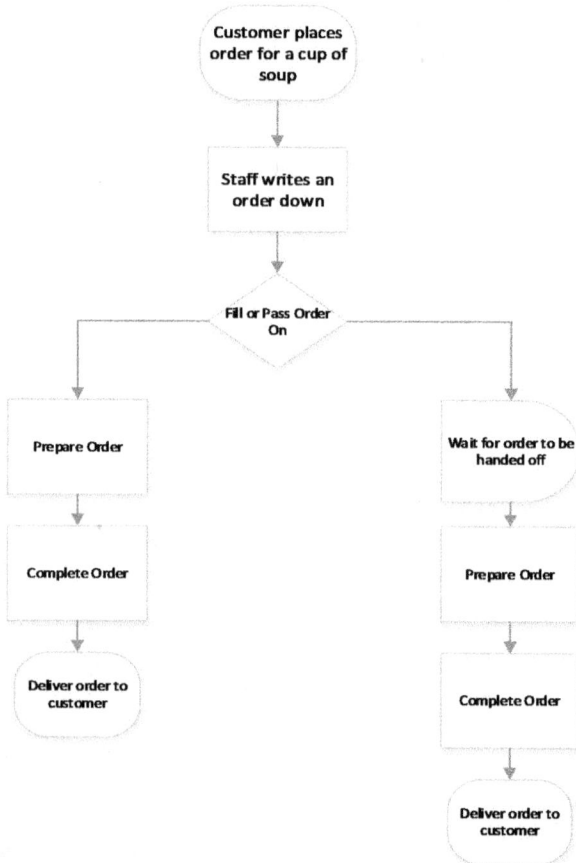

Checklist or Check Sheet

Purpose: Generally used in conjunction with inspection to capture the results of visual observations.

RANGE OF MEASUREMENTS	FREQUENCY
0.990-0.995 INCHES	////
0.996-1.000 INCHES	﷼﷼
1.001-1.005 INCHES	﷼﷼ ////
1.006-1.010 INCHES	﷼﷼ ﷼﷼ //
1.011-1.015 INCHES	////
1.016-1.020 INCHES	//

Pareto Chart

Purpose: Used to identify the top issues. Based on the 80/20 rule which states 80% of the problems are caused by 20% of the reasons.

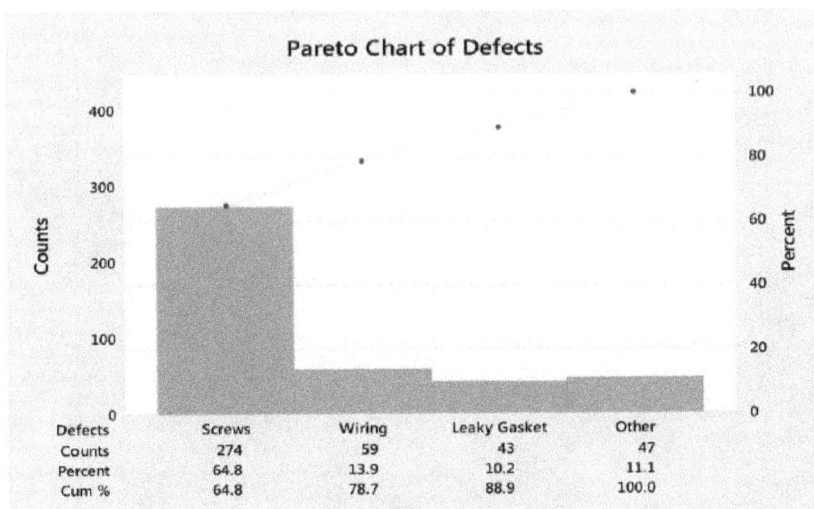

Pareto Chart of Defects

Defects	Screws	Wiring	Leaky Gasket	Other
Counts	274	59	43	47
Percent	64.8	13.9	10.2	11.1
Cum %	64.8	78.7	88.9	100.0

Histogram

Purpose: Show the relative frequency of a variable.

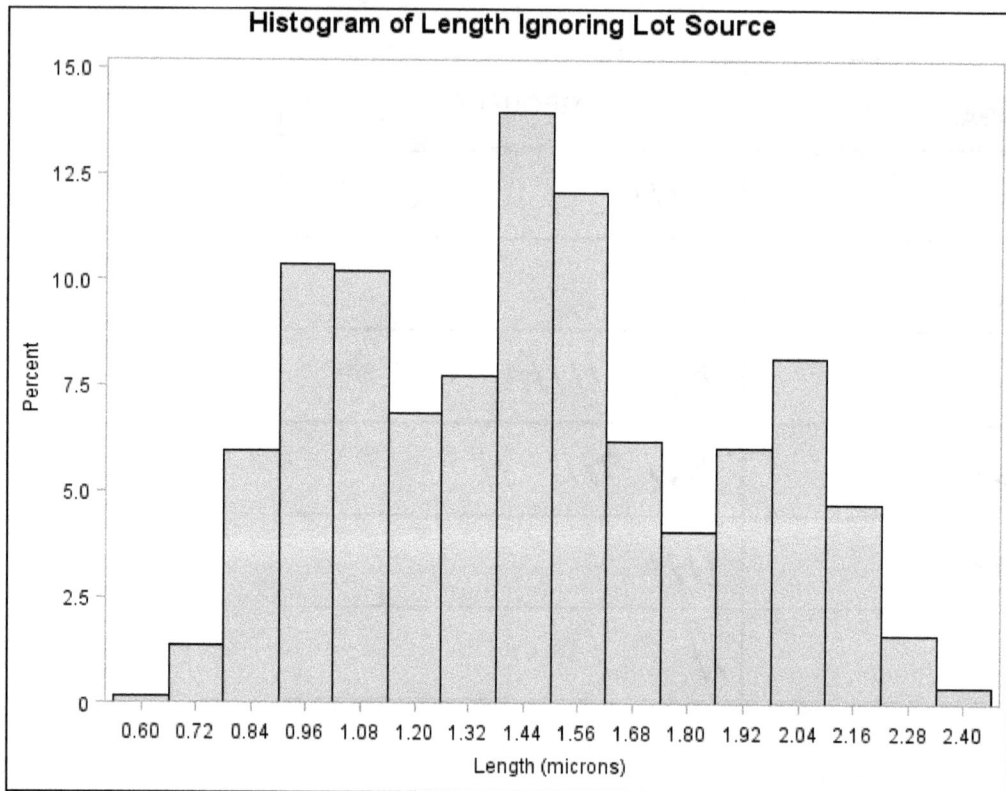

Histogram of Length Ignoring Lot Source

Scatter Diagram

Purpose: Used to determine if two variables impact one another.

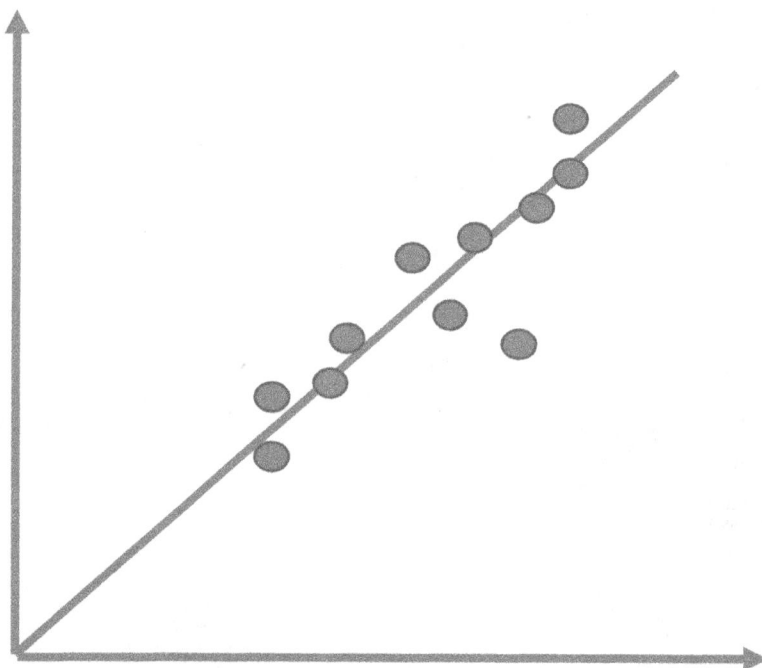

Control Chart (a type of run chart)

Purpose: Used to determine if a process is within statistical control. It uses the Rule of 7 which states 7 or more data points in a row above or below the statistical mean indicates a process out of control.

Common Causes are causes that are generally difficult to determine. They exist within the upper and lower control limits.

Special Causes of Variation are causes that are generally easy to discern. A special cause is generally represented by a data point outside of the control limits.

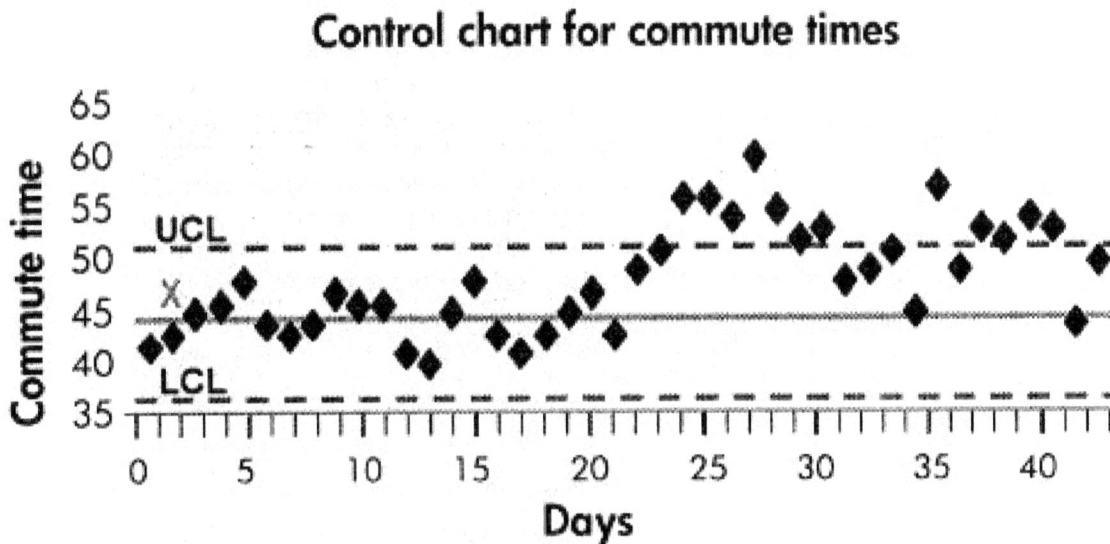

A control chart is a type of run chart but a run chart does not include the upper and lower control limits.

Quality Theories

Quality Theory	Theory
Total Quality Management	An integrated management philosophy posited by Feigenbaum, around quality and continuous improvement that states that everyone in the organization is responsible for quality. It integrates the concept of quality into the culture of an organizations.
Kaizen (Change for Better)	A philosophy posited by Kaoru Ishikawa that looks for small and continuous improvements in the processes that organizations undertake. All employees of the company are involved in proactivity working towards achieving regular, incremental improvements to the project. It requires all of the employees to be actively engaged in finding areas of improvement. Kaizen uses the Plan – Do – Check – Act cycle to provide a scientific approach to improvements in the organization. A typical
Kanban	Kanban is Japanese for "card" or "visual signal" and is used to provide a visual overview of the manufacturing process. In general, Kanban uses a pull-based inventory management system based on the principle of just-in-time (JIT) in conjunction with the visualization of work and the workflow.
Deming Cycle (Plan – Do – Check – Act)	The Demining Wheel, a theory by W. Edward Deming, provides a continuous cycle where a change is planned (develop a hypothesis), we do the change (run the experiment), check or evaluate the results, and then act based on the outcome by refining your experiment and then starting a new cycle. It is also referred to as the Deming-Shewhart chart. This methodology is often used in conjunction with philosophies of Kaizen in organizations
Conformance to Requirements	A theory by Philip Crosby where quality is achieved when the product conforms to requirements. Quality is achieved by prevention, not appraisal.
Design of Experiments	Design of Experiments, also known as the Taguchi method is a systematic method of determining the relationship between factors affecting the process or the output of the process. It looks for cause and effect type relationships.

Earned Value Formulas

Name	Definition	Formula	Interpretation
Planned Value (PV)	Scheduled work for authorized budget. It identifies the value of the work we planned to have completed at a point in time.	EV = sum of the of completed work planned value	
Earned Value (EV)	A measure of the work completed in relation to the terms of the budget authorized for the work.		
Actual Cost (AC)	The actual cost of the work completed at a point in time.		
Budget at Completion (BAC)	The sum of the budgets established to perform the work. It is the value of all planned work.		
Cost Variance	The difference in the value of the work completed at a point in time. It calculates the amount of the budget deficit or surplus.	$CV = EV - AC$	Positive - under cost Neutral – on cost Negative – over cost
Schedule Variance	The difference in the work planned to be completed at a point in time and the work actually completed at a point in time. It calculates the schedule deficit or surplus.	$SV = EV - PV$	Positive - ahead of schedule Neutral – on planned schedule Negative – behind schedule

Name	Definition	Formula	Interpretation
Variance at Completion (VAC)	VAC calculates the estimated difference in cost at the completion of the project. It is expressed as a difference between BAC and ETC.	$VAC = BAC - EAC$	Positive - under cost Neutral – on cost Negative – over cost
Cost Performance Index (CPI)	A measure of cost efficiency. It looks at EV and AC and is expressed as a ratio.	$CPI = \dfrac{EV}{AC}$	>1.0 = Under cost =1.0 = On cost <1.0 = Over cost Ex: CPI = .86, we are earning 0.86 cents of value for every dollar spent.
Schedule Performance Index (SPI)	A measure of schedule efficiency. It looks at EV and PV and is expressed as a ratio.	$SPI = \dfrac{EV}{PV}$	>1.0 = Under planned schedule =1.0 = On planned schedule <1.0 = Over planned schedule Ex: SPI = .86, we are proceeding at the 86% of the rate originally planned.

Estimate at Completion (EAC)	The total cost of completing all work represented as the sum of the actual costs and the ETC. There are four formulas to know.		
	If CPI is expected to stay the same.	$EAC = \dfrac{BAC}{CPI}$	
	If future work will be accomplished at the planned rate.	$EAC = AC + BAC - EV$	
	If the initial plan is no longer valid.	$EAC = Ac + bottom\ up\ ETC$	
	If both CPI and SPI will influence remaining work.	$EAC = AC + \dfrac{(BAC - EV)}{(CPI\ x\ SPI)}$	

Estimate to Complete (ETC)	Cost expected to finish all remaining project work. There are two formulas to know.		
	Assuming work is proceeding on plan.	$ETC = EAC - AC$	
	Re-estimate remaining work from the bottom up.	$ETC = Reestimate$	

Name	Definition	Formula	Interpretation
To Complete Performance Index (TCPI)	A measure of cost performance to achieve with remaining resources to reach a specific goal.		>1.0 = Harder to Complete
	Efficiency to maintain in order to complete on plan.	$TCPI = \dfrac{(BAC - EV)}{(BAC - AC)}$	=1.0 = Same to Complete
	Efficiency to maintain to complete current EAC.	$TCPI = \dfrac{(BAC - EV)}{(EAC - AC)}$	<1.0 = Easier to Complete

Network Diagram Mapping

Day 0 Start – AoN Formula Map

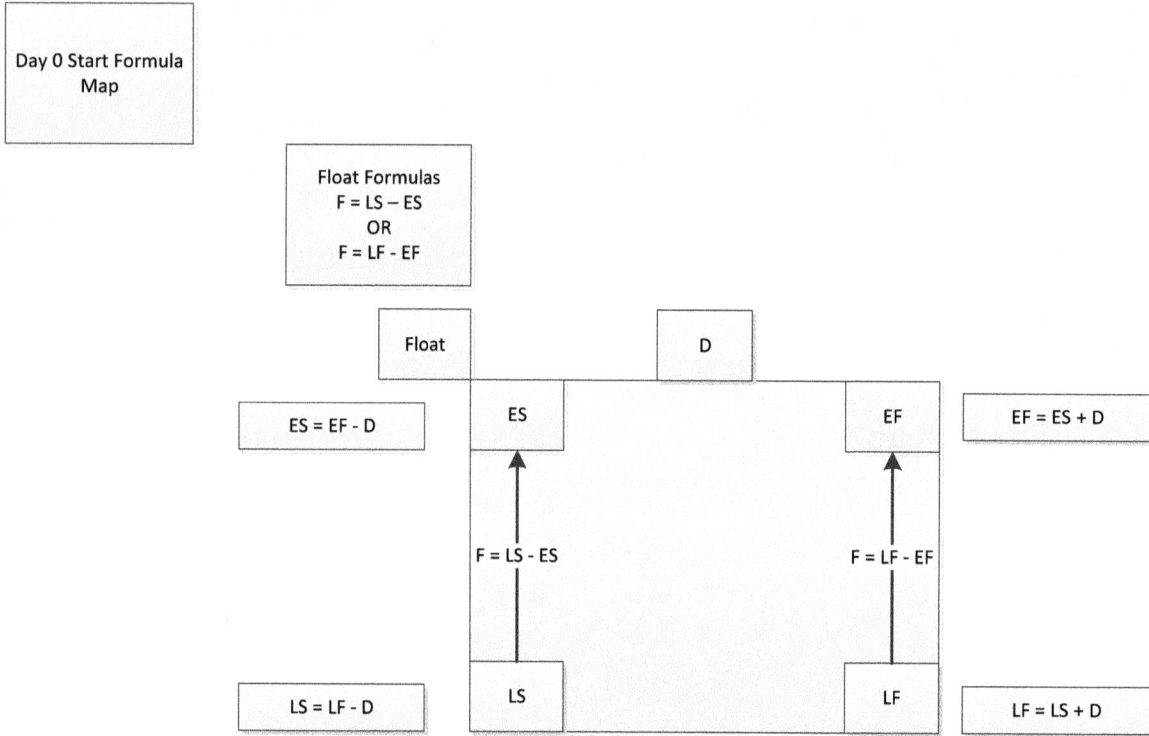

Day 0 Start Formula Map

Float Formulas
$F = LS - ES$
OR
$F = LF - EF$

Float

D

ES = EF - D

ES

EF

EF = ES + D

$F = LS - ES$

$F = LF - EF$

LS = LF - D

LS

LF

LF = LS + D

Day 1 Start – (AoN) Formula Map (most common)

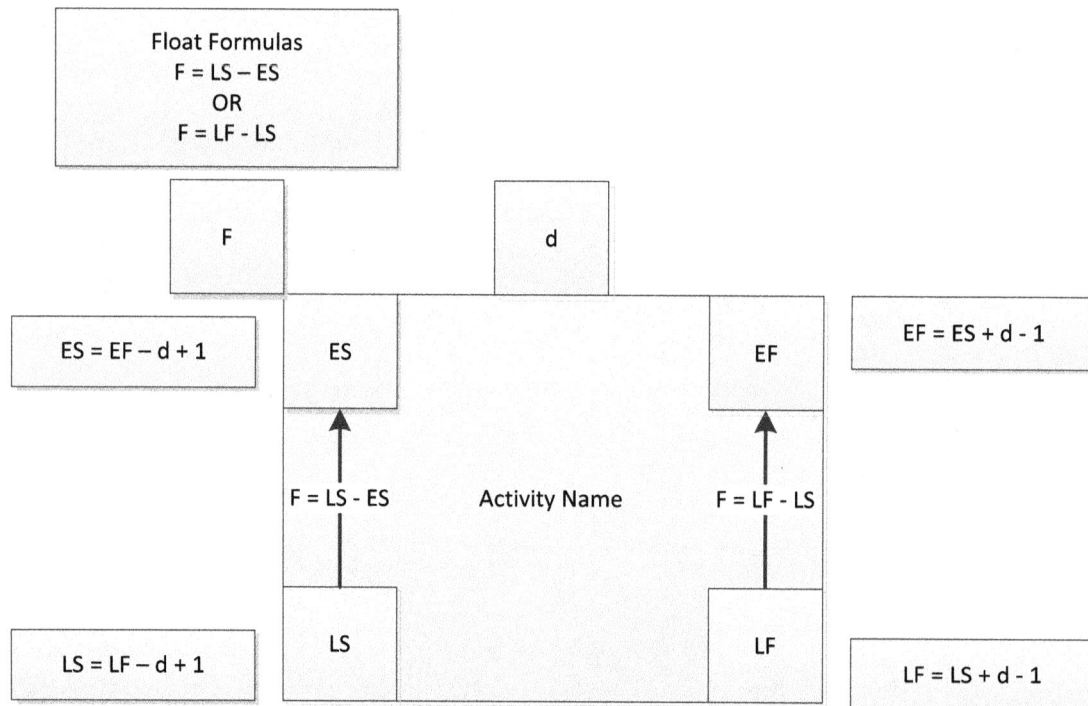

Float Formulas
$F = LS - ES$
OR
$F = LF - LS$

F

d

ES = EF − d + 1

ES

EF

EF = ES + d - 1

$F = LS - ES$

Activity Name

$F = LF - LS$

LS = LF − d + 1

LS

LF

LF = LS + d - 1

Network Diagram Types

Activity on Node

Activity on Node – (Common, know how to complete for exam)

Shows 4 relationships

- Start to Start
- Start to Finish
- Finish to Start
- Finish to Finish

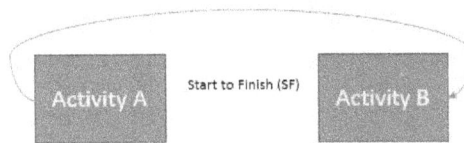

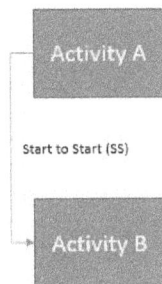

Activity on Arrow

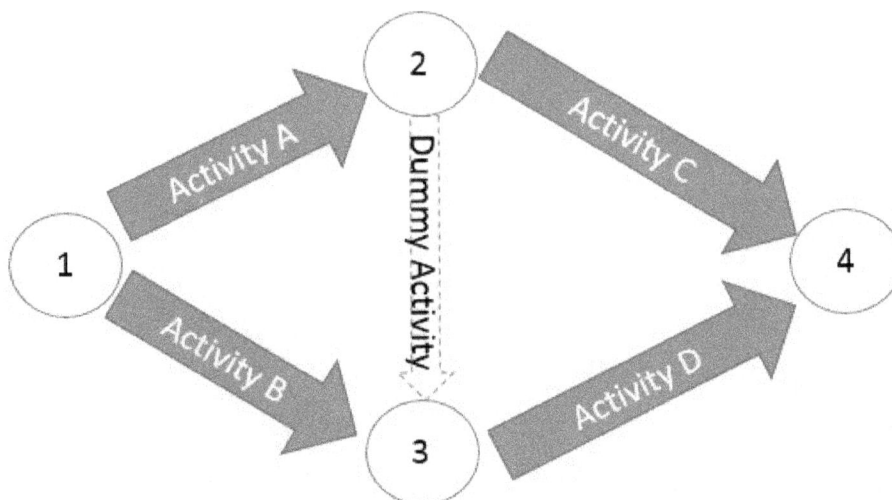

Activity on Arrow – (Less common, know concept based questions)

Shows 1 relationship type, the Finish to Start Relationship

Schedule Compression Impact

Schedule Compression Technique	General Impact
Fast Track	• Adds risk • Increase management time
Crash	• Adds costs • Increases management time
Reduce Scope	• Decreases time and cost • Increases customers dissatisfaction
Cut Quality	• Decreases cost and resources • Increases risk
Resource Reallocations	• Neither adds cost nor increases risk

Gantt Chart / PDM Relationships

Finish-to-Start (FS) Relationship

Finish-to-Start

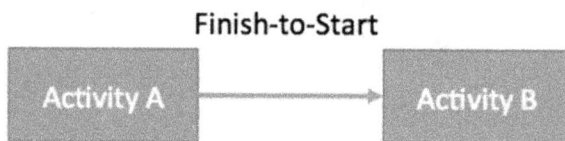

Activity A must finish before Activity B can start.

Finish-to-Finish (FF) Relationship

Finish-to-Finish

Activity A must finish before Activity B can finish.

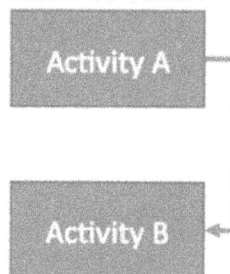

Start-to-Start (SS) Relationship

Start-to-Start

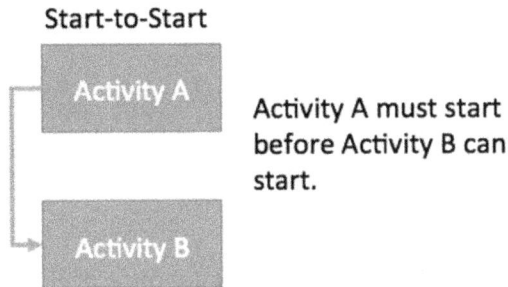

Activity A must start before Activity B can start.

Start-to-Finish (SF) Relationship

Start-to-Finish

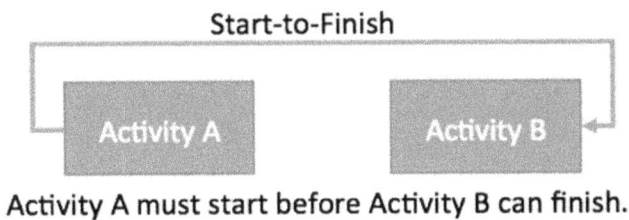

Activity A must start before Activity B can finish.

Sample Gantt Chart

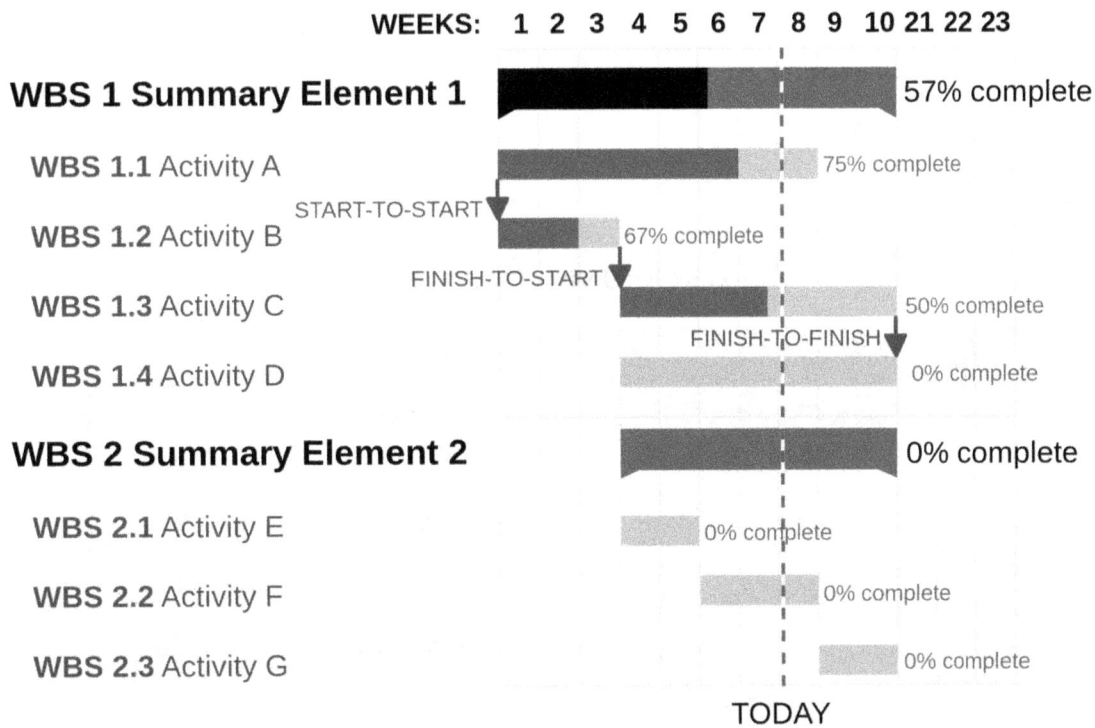

WEEKS:	1 2 3 4 5 6 7 8 9 10 21 22 23	

WBS 1 Summary Element 1 — 57% complete

WBS **1.1** Activity A — 75% complete

START-TO-START

WBS **1.2** Activity B — 67% complete

FINISH-TO-START

WBS **1.3** Activity C — 50% complete

FINISH-TO-FINISH

WBS **1.4** Activity D — 0% complete

WBS 2 Summary Element 2 — 0% complete

WBS **2.1** Activity E — 0% complete

WBS **2.2** Activity F — 0% complete

WBS **2.3** Activity G — 0% complete

TODAY

Risk Calculations

Risk Formulas

Risk Weight = Risk Probability * Risk Impact

Expected Value = Probability of Outcome x $ Impact of Outcome

Make or Buy Analysis Formula:

Upfront Cost to Make + (Maintenance of Make Cost x Y) = Upfront Cost to Buy + (Maintenance of Buy Cost x Y)

Where Y is the duration at which the cost of making the product equals the cost of buying (the break even point)

Decision Tree

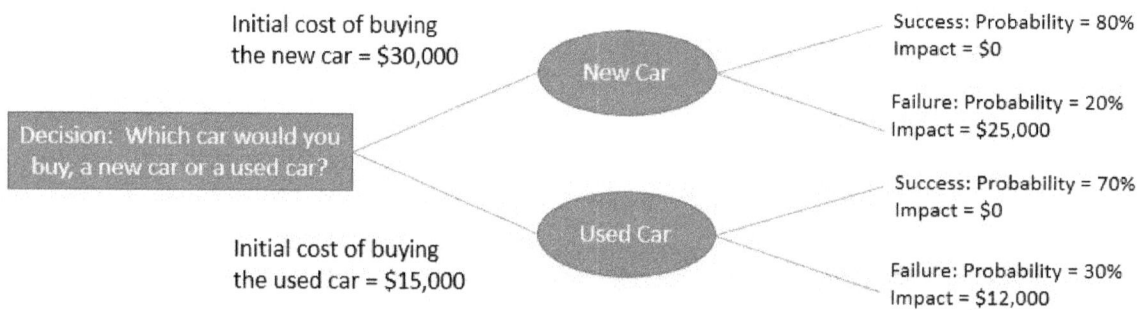

Expected Monetary Value

Calculate the expected monetary value (EMV) for the given work packages:

Work Package	Probability	Impact	Expected Monetary Value
A	15%	+$20,000	-$3,000
B	25%	-$4,000	-$1,000
C	10%	-$35,000	+$3,500
		Total EMV:	-$500

Risk Response Strategies

Positive Risk Strategies	Negative Risk Strategies
Exploit	Avoid
Enhance	Transfer
Share	Mitigate
Accept	Accept

Probability Basics

Event	Probability Calculation
P(A) and P(A') are complements	$P(A) + P(A') = 1$
P(A or B)	$P(A) + P(B) - P(A \text{ and } B)$
P(A and B) for Independent Events	$P(A) \times P(B)$
P(A or B) for Mutually Exclusive Events	$P(A) + P(B)$

Contract Types

Contract Type	Advantages	Disadvantages	Who Bears the Risk?
Cost Plus	Lower cost than fixed price Simple to draft Seller does not account for risk	All seller invoices audited, increasing buyer effort Less incentive for seller to control costs Less Efficient for buyer	Buyer
Time and Material	Easy to create Good for resource augmentation	No incentive for seller to control costs Requires daily monitoring of output Not good for large, complex projects	Shared by Buyer and Seller
Fixed Price	• More efficient for buyer • Seller has incentive to control costs • Requires less effort by buyer	Seller may try to make margins through changes Unclear SOW can result in missing deliverables	Seller

Cost Plus (a/k/a Cost Reimbursable)

- Seller paid based on actual costs

- Plus may have an incentive fee or fixed fee

- 4 Main Cost Plus Contracts

    - Cost Plus Fee (CPF) or Cost Plus Fixed Fee (CPFF)

    - Cost Plus Inventive Fee (CPIF)

    - Cost Plus Award Fee (CPAF)

    - Cost Plus Percentage of Costs (CPPC)

Time and Material (a/k/a Unit Price)

- Used for smaller projects or to supplement larger projects

- Pay per item, per hour, or per day

    - Pay for cost of material

    - Pay for Labor (Time)

Lump Sum (a/k/a Fixed Price)

- Used when scope is very clear

- Seller paid a fixed price

- 3 Main Lump Sum Contracts

    - Firm Fixed Price (FFP)

    - Fixed Price Incentive Fee (FPIF)

    - Fix Price – Economic Price Adjusted (FP-EPA)

Contract Formulas

Contract Costs	Formula
Incentive / Bonus to Seller	$(Target\ Cost - Actual\ Cost)x\ Seller\ \%\ of\ Cost\ Savings$
Final Contract Cost / Fee or Overhead (Given to seller)	$Target\ Fee + Incentive$
Total Cost/Price of Procurement	$Actual\ Cost + Final\ Contract\ Cost$
Point of Total Assumption for Cost Reimbursable Contracts	$Target\ Cost + \dfrac{Ceiling\ Price - (Target\ Cost + Fixed\ Fees))}{Benefit\ Share}$
Point of Total Assumption for Fixed Price Contracts	$Target\ Cost + \dfrac{(Ceiling\ Price - Target\ Price)}{Benefit\ Share}$

Cost Plus Fixed Fee

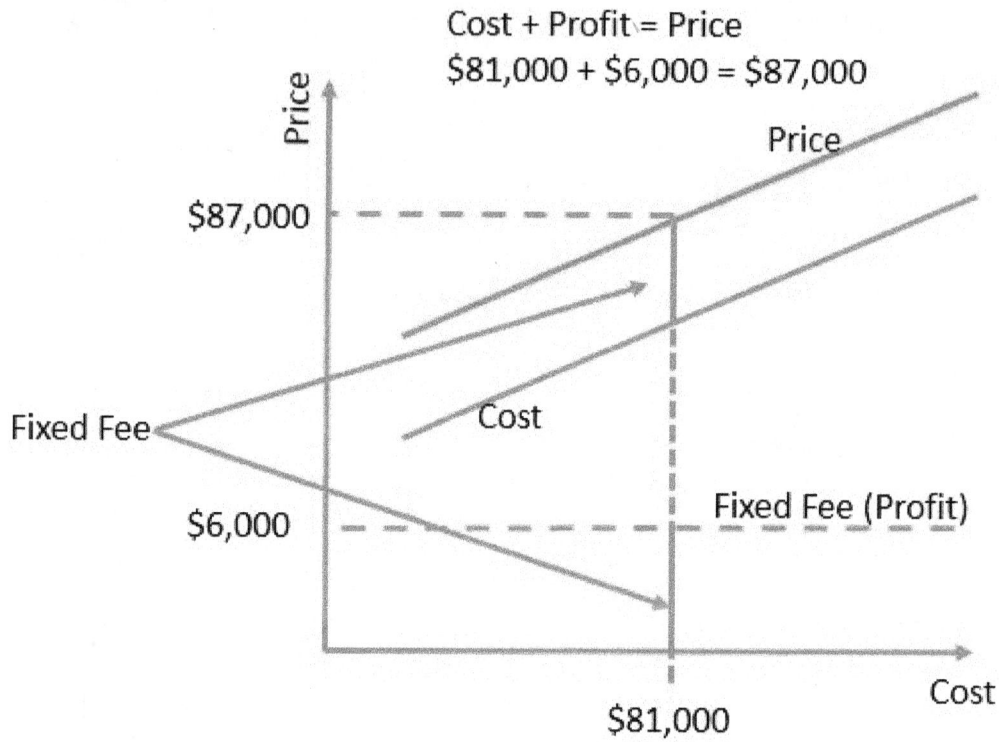

Cost + Profit = Price
$81,000 + $6,000 = $87,000

Price

Price

$87,000

Fixed Fee

Cost

Fixed Fee (Profit)

$6,000

Cost

$81,000

Cost Plus Incentive Fee

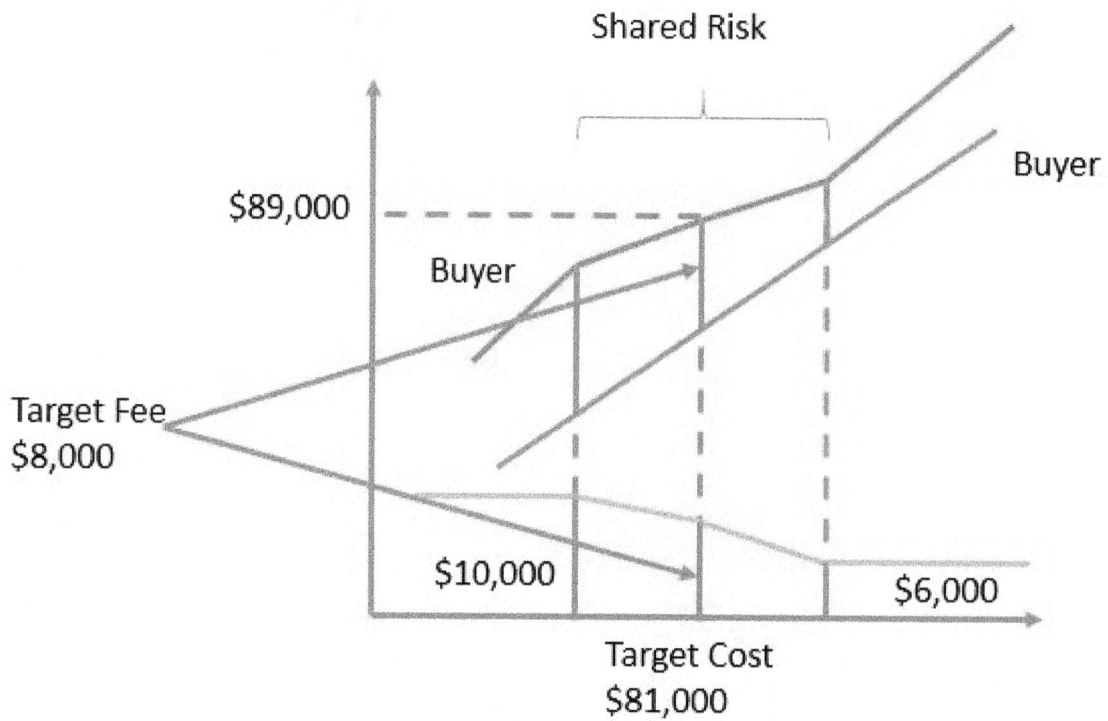

Shared Risk

Buyer

$89,000

Buyer

Target Fee
$8,000

$10,000

$6,000

Target Cost
$81,000

Firm Fixed Fee

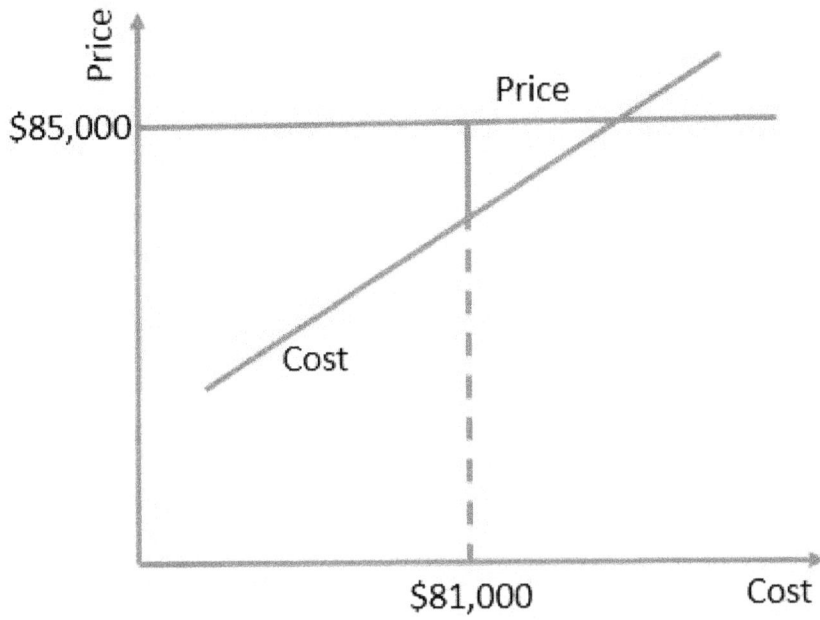

Fixed Price Incentive Fee

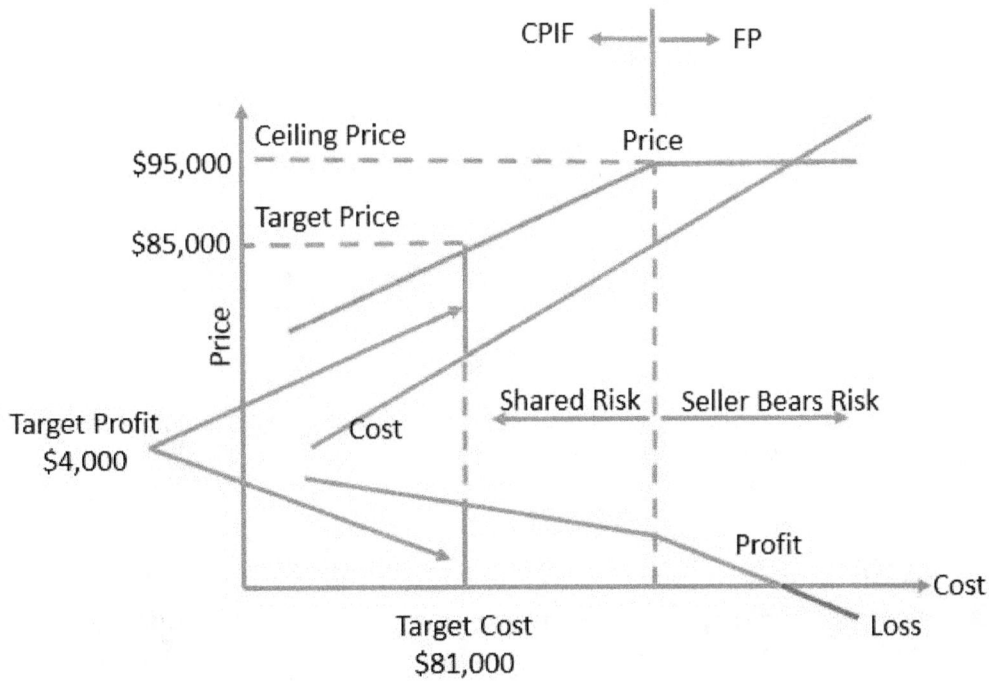

Fixed Price

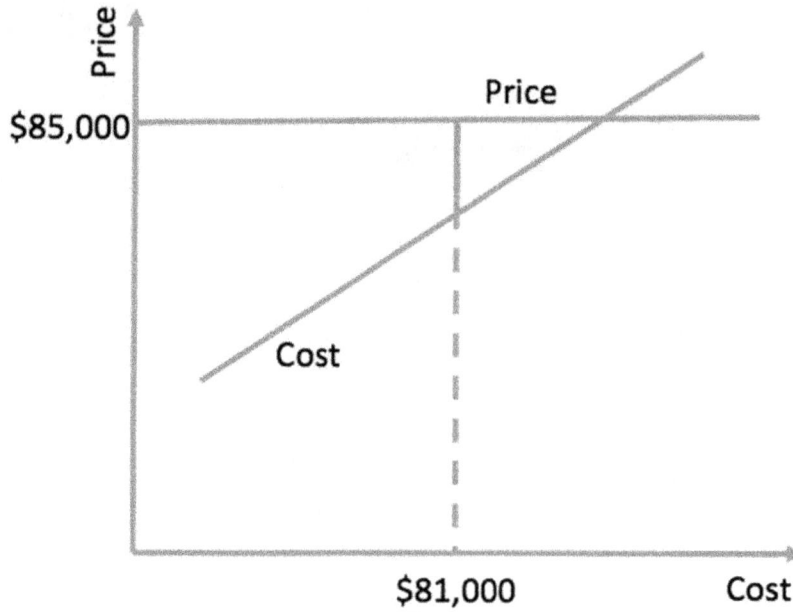

Point of Total Assumption

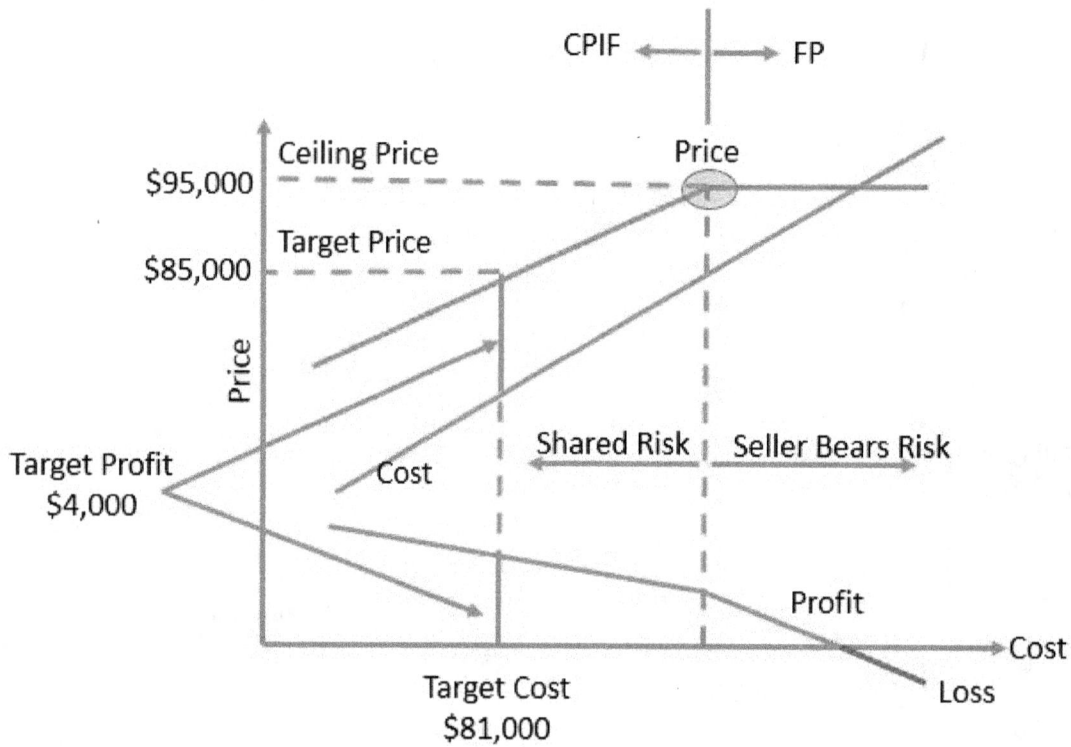

Stakeholder Classification Models

4 models:

- Power/interest grid
- Power/influence grid
- Influence/Impact grid
- Salience model (power/urgency/legitimacy)

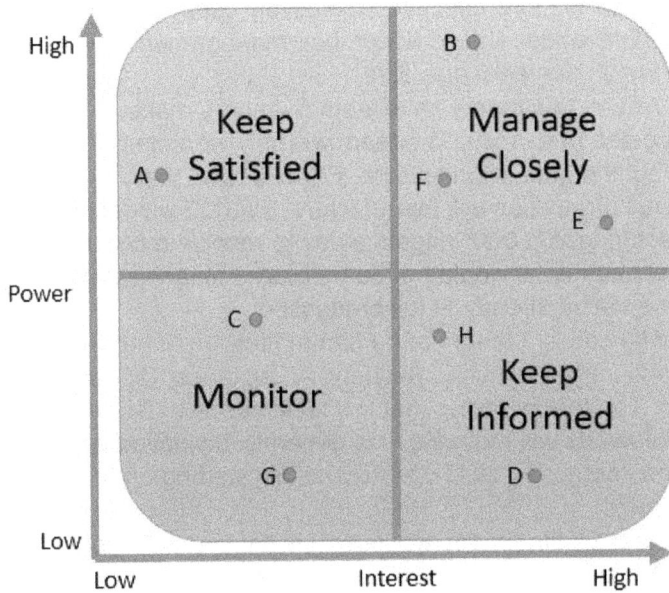

Stakeholder Engagement Assessment Matrix

Stakeholder	Unaware	Resistant	Neutral	Supportive	Leading
Stakeholder 1	C		D		
Stakeholder 2			C	D	
Stakeholder 3					C, D

C = Current State
D = Desired State

Organizational Theories

Organizational Theory	Description
Contingency Theory	Developed by Fred E. Fielder, it states a leader's effectiveness contingent on two sets of factors. The first set of factors look at if the leader is task-oriented or relationship-oriented. The second set of factors evaluations situational factors in the workplace. In practical application, a task-oriented leader is more effective in stressful environments and the relationship oriented leader is more effective in relatively calm environments. An effective leader should adapt their management style to the environment in which the team operates.
Expectancy Theory	Developed by Victor Vroom, this theory says team members make choices based on expected outcomes. The team will only work hard toward a goal if they feel the goal is achievable. For example, if a manufacturing line at full production will manufacture 100,000 widgets a day, a goal of manufacturing 200,000 widgets a day to receive a bonus will not be motivational because it would not be perceived as achievable on a manufacturing line that is already at full production.
Maslow's Hierarchy of Needs	Maslow's Hierarchy of Needs is a theory of human motivation. It groups needs into five categories: Physiological, Security, Acceptance, Esteem, and Self-Actualization. The theory states that low level needs must be met before higher level needs will motivate. It is generally displayed as a pyramid to illustrate the categories build on one another starting on the lowest level of the pyramid.
McGregor's Theory X and Theory Y	McGregor's Theory X and Y categorizes workers in two ways. A Theory X manager assumes the team members are unmotivated and much be micro managed and forced to work. Constant supervision is necessary to complete the project. Theory Y managers view workers as self-motivated and do not need external motivation. In this environment, the manager takes a laissez faire or hands off policy of management.
Herzberg's Motivation-Hygiene Theory	Herzberg classified motivational factors into Hygiene Factors and Motivation Factors. This theory states that Motivation factors will not motivate if the hygiene factors are not met. Additionally, the hygiene factors by themselves will not motivate, but the absence of these factors can make the worker unsatisfied and less motivated. Company policies, supervision, working conditions, paycheck, work-life balance, status, security are examples of Hygiene factors. Achievement, responsibility, advancement, and growth are all examples of Motivation factors.
McClelland's Three Need Theory	McClelland's Three Need Theory says people are motivated based on three primary needs: Achievement, Power, and Affiliation. A team member with a high need for achievement needs to stand out from the group and will gravitate towards others with a high need for achievement. A need for power is generally a need to social (institutional) power or personal power. A need for social power is generally more effective than a need for personal power. The third category of affiliation says individuals want to belong to a team and will work to maintain their relationships. This theory may also be referred to as Achievement Theory or McClelland's Theory of Needs.

Stages of Team Formation

Phase where the team meets and starts to learn about their role and the project.

Team members start to adjust their working style and habits to the team. Trust develops.

Team completes work and are released from the project.

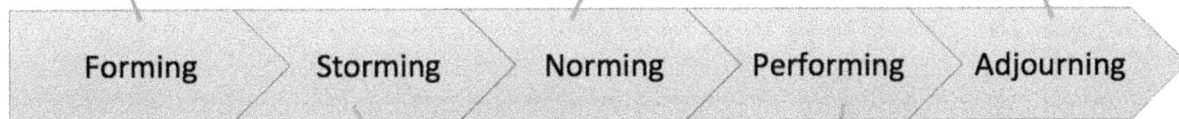

Forming → Storming → Norming → Performing → Adjourning

Team starts addressing project work and making decisions, and disagreements may emerge.

Team starts delivering on the project and work together as an organized unit.

Forms of Power

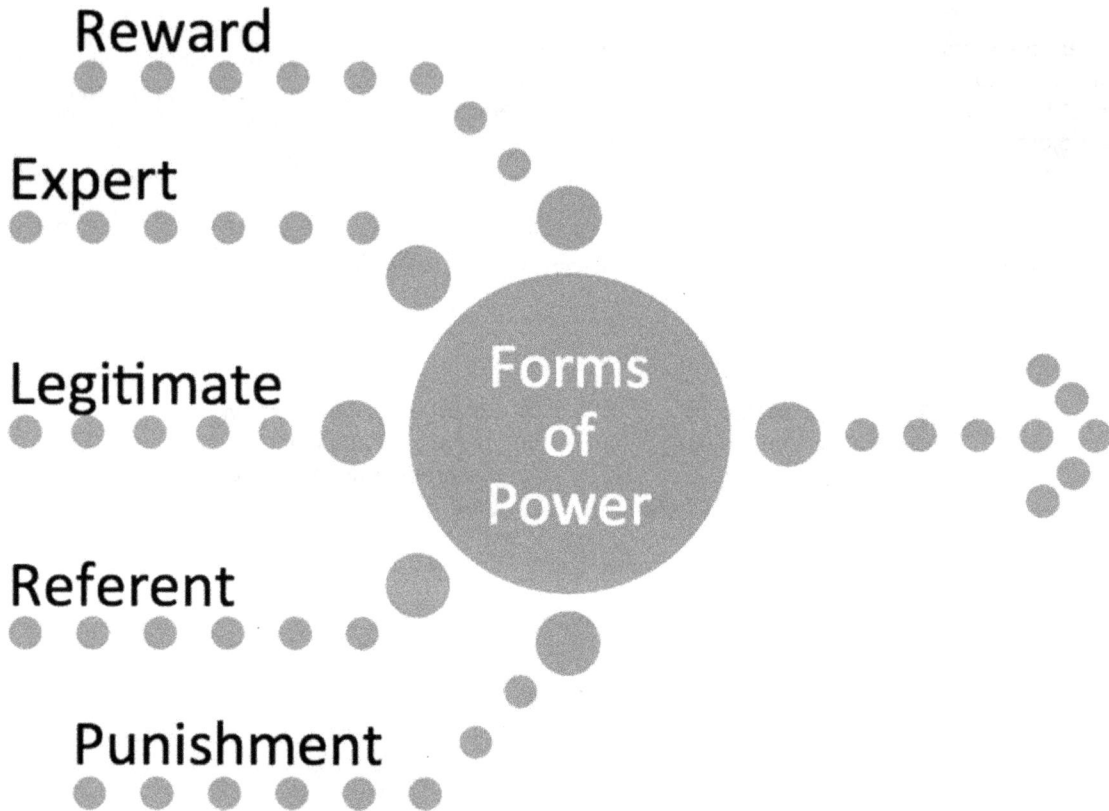

Reward

Expert

Legitimate

Referent

Punishment

Forms of Power

Form of Power	Definition
Reward	Reward is the ability to give a reward or recognition.
Expert	Expert power is power based on expertise in a subject area.
Legitimate	Legitimate power is power derived from a position within an organization.
Reference	Referent Power is the power gained by respect for or charisma of a manager.
Penalty	Punishment power is the power to assess a penalty for not meeting a goal. It is also referred to as coercive power.

Best Forms of Power: Reward and Expert

Worst Form of Power: Penalty

Conflict Resolution Techniques

Conflict Resolution Technique	Definition
Collaborate or Problem solve	Collaborating or problem solving looks at incorporating multiple viewpoints into the solution. It generally encourages open dialog and consensus.
Smooth or Accommodate	Smooth or accommodate involves emphasizing areas where stakeholders may agree rather than areas where they disagree. One person may concede their position to maintain the relationship.
Compromise or Reconcile	Searching for a solution that is agreeable to all parties. It usually involves each party giving up something to resolve the conflict.
Withdraw or Avoid	Withdraw or avoid involves removing yourself from the conflict to postpone the issue to allow for investigation and information gathering.
Force or Direct	Force or direct involves forcing a viewpoint and offers a win-lose situation and can originate from a power position.

Sources of Conflict

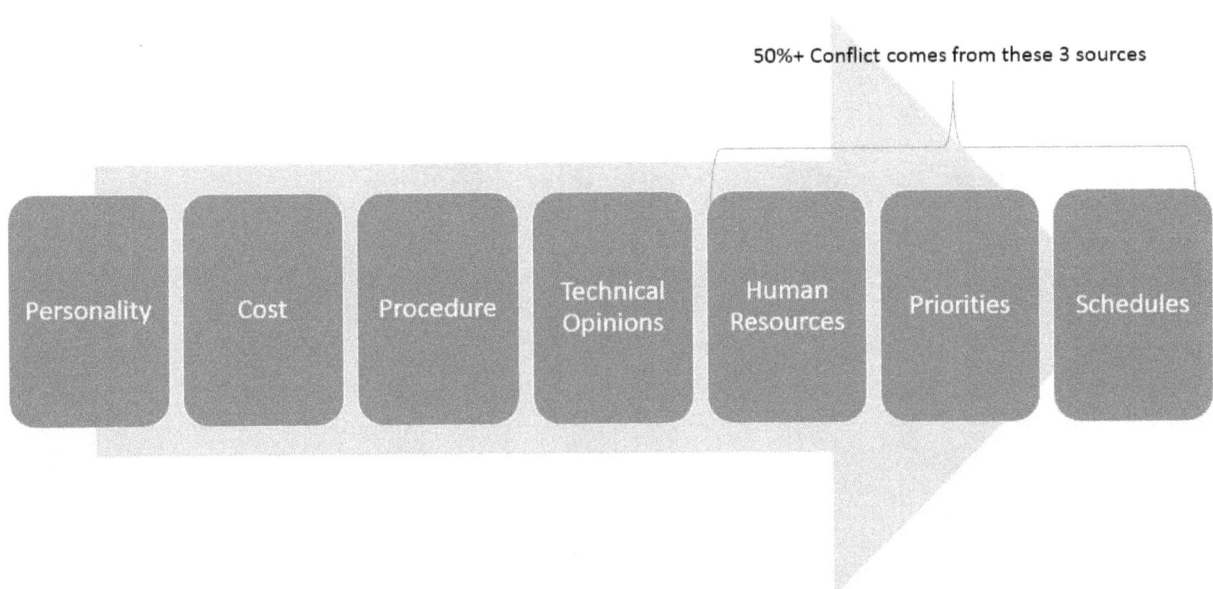

50%+ Conflict comes from these 3 sources

Personality   Cost   Procedure   Technical Opinions   Human Resources   Priorities   Schedules

Basic Communication Model

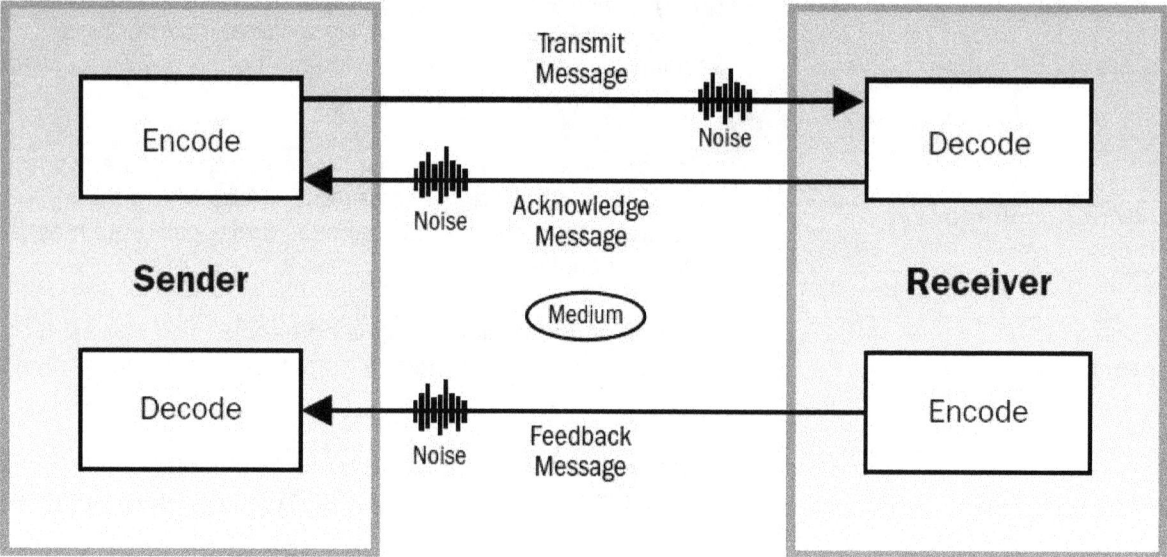

Diagram: Sender box contains **Encode** and **Decode** blocks; Receiver box contains **Decode** and **Encode** blocks. Arrows — Transmit Message (Sender Encode → Receiver Decode), Acknowledge Message (Receiver Decode → Sender Encode), Feedback Message (Receiver Encode → Sender Decode) — each passing through **Noise**. A **Medium** oval sits in the center.

Group Creativity Techniques

Technique	Definition
Brainstorming	Brainstorming is used to generate and collect a large number of ideas. It generally does not involve analyzing, critiquing, or prioritizing information.
Nominal Group Technique	Nominal Group Technique enhances brainstorming by adding a voting process for ranking the most useful ideas for further analysis.
Idea/Mind Mapping	Ideas generated in individual brainstorming sessions are consolidated into a single map in a manner that groups similar ideas.
Affinity Diagram	Allows a large number of ideas to be classified into groups for further analysis.
Multi Criteria Decision Analysis	Uses a decision matrix to provide a systematic method of generating ideas using established criteria.

Group Decision Making Techniques

Technique	Definition
Unanimity	A decision is reached when everyone agrees on a single course of action. The Delphi Technique is a method for gaining unanimity using questionnaires to anonymously attain feedback from subject matter experts.
Majority	A decision is reached when more than 50% of a group agree on the course of action.
Plurality	A decision is reached based on the agreement of the largest block in a group. This method is generally used when there are more than 2 potential solutions.
Dictatorship	One person makes the decision for the group.

Ethical Decision Making Framework

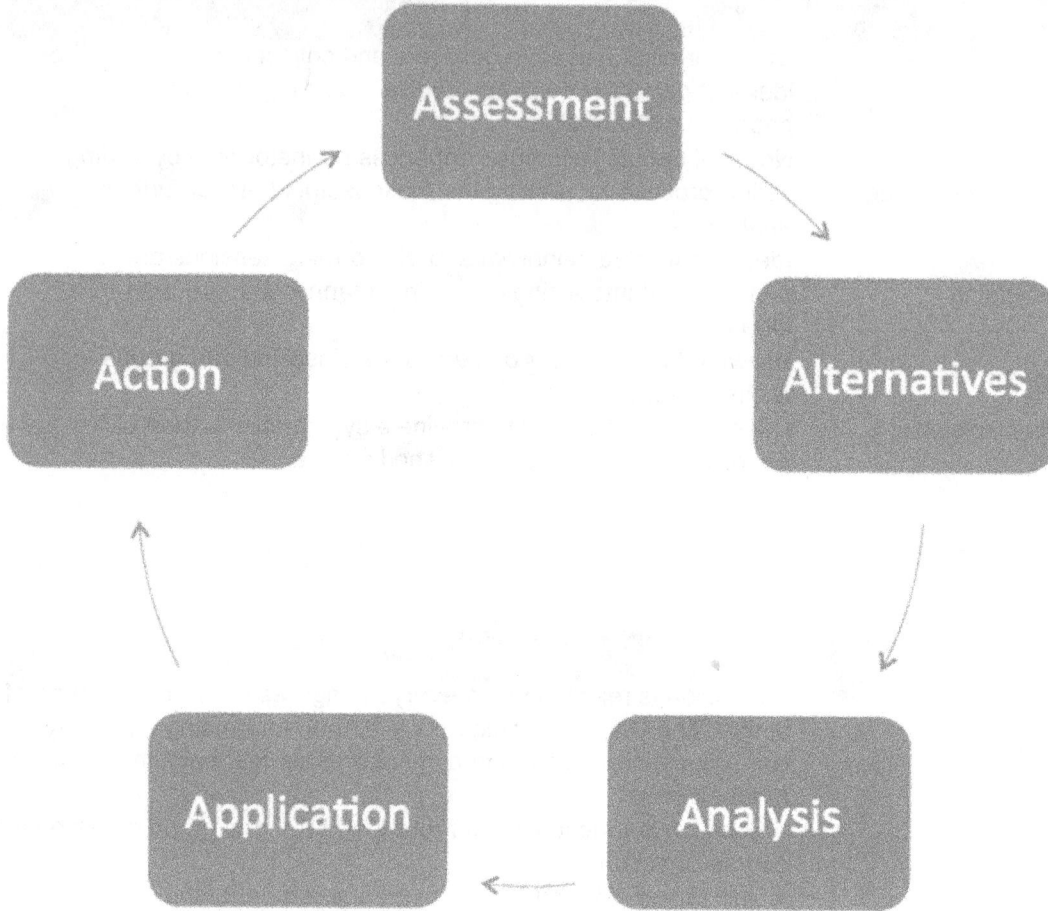

A cyclical diagram showing five connected stages: Assessment, Alternatives, Analysis, Application, and Action, with arrows flowing clockwise from Assessment → Alternatives → Analysis → Application → Action → back to Assessment.

Inputs, Tools & Techniques, and Outputs

Project Integration Management Knowledge Area

Develop Project Charter		
Inputs	**Tools & Techniques**	**Outputs**
Project Statement of Work	Expert Judgment	Project Charter
Business Case	Facilitation Techniques	
Agreements		
Enterprise Environmental Factors		
Organizational Process Assets		

Develop Project Management Plan		
Inputs	**Tools & Techniques**	**Outputs**
Project Charter	Expert Judgment	Project Management Plan
Outputs from Other Processes	Facilitation Techniques	
Enterprise Environmental Factors		
Organizational Process Assets		

Direct and Manage Project Work		
Inputs	**Tools & Techniques**	**Outputs**
Project Management Plan	Expert Judgment	Deliverables
Approved Change Requests	Project Management Information System	Work Performance Data
Enterprise Environmental Factors	Meetings	Change Requests
Organizational Process Assets		Project Management Plan Updates
		Project Document Updates

Monitor and Control Project Work

Inputs	Tools & Techniques	Outputs
Project Management Plan	Expert Judgment	Change Requests
Schedule Forecasts	Analytical Techniques	Work Performance Reports
Cost Forecasts	Project Management Information System	Project Management Plan Updates
Validated Changes	Meetings	Project Document Updates
Work Performance Information		
Enterprise Environmental Factors		
Organizational Process Assets		

Perform Integrated Change Control

Inputs	Tools & Techniques	Outputs
Project Management Plan	Expert Judgment	Approved Change Requests
Work Performance Reports	Meetings	Change Log
Change Requests	Change Control Tools	Project Management Plan Updates
Enterprise Environmental Factors		Project Document Updates
Organizational Process Assets		

Close Project or Phase

Inputs	Tools & Techniques	Outputs
Project Management Plan	Expert Judgment	Final Product, Service, or Result Transition
Accepted Deliverables	Analytical Techniques	Organization Process Assets Updates
Organizational Process Assets	Meetings	

Plan Scope Management		
Inputs	**Tools & Techniques**	**Outputs**
Project Management Plan	Expert Judgment	Scope Management Plan
Project Charter	Meetings	Requirements Management Plan
Enterprise Environmental Factors		
Organizational Process Assets		

Collect Requirements		
Inputs	**Tools & Techniques**	**Outputs**
Scope Management Plan	Interviews	Requirements Documentation
Requirements Management Plan	Focus Groups	Requirements Traceability Matrix
Stakeholder Management Plan	Facilitated Workshops	
Project Charter	Group Creativity Techniques	
Stakeholder Register	Group Decision-Making Techniques	
	Questionnaires and Surveys	
	Observations	
	Prototypes	
	Benchmarking	
	Context Diagrams	
	Document Analysis	

Define Scope		
Inputs	**Tools & Techniques**	**Outputs**
Scope Management Plan	Expert Judgment	Project Scope Statement
Project Charter	Product Analysis	Project Document Updates
Requirements Documentation	Alternatives Generation	
Organizational Process Assets	Facilitated Workshops	

Create WBS		
Inputs	**Tools & Techniques**	**Outputs**
Scope Management Plan	Decomposition	Scope Baseline
Project Scope Statement	Expert Judgment	Project Document Updates
Requirements Documentation		
Enterprise Environmental Factors		
Organizational Process Assets		

Validate Scope		
Inputs	**Tools & Techniques**	**Outputs**
Project Management Plan	Inspection	Accepted Deliverables
Requirements Documentation	Group Decision-Making Techniques	Change Requests
Requirements Traceability Matrix		Work Performance Information
Verified Deliverables		Project Documents Updates
Work Performance Data		

Control Scope		
Inputs	**Tools & Techniques**	**Outputs**
Project Management Plan	Variance Analysis	Work Performance Information
Requirements Documentation		Change Requests
Requirements Traceability Matrix		Project Management Plan Updates
Work Performance Data		Project Documents Updates
Organizational Process Assets		Organization Process Assets Updates

Plan Schedule Management		
Inputs	**Tools & Techniques**	**Outputs**
Project Management Plan	Expert Judgment	Schedule Management Plan
Project Charter	Analytical Techniques	
Enterprise Environmental Factors	Meetings	
Organizational Process Assets		

Define Activities		
Inputs	**Tools & Techniques**	**Outputs**
Schedule Management Plan	Decomposition	Activity List
Scope Baseline	Rolling Wave Planning	Activity Attributes
Enterprise Environmental Factors	Expert Judgment	Milestones List
Organizational Process Assets		

Sequence Activities		
Inputs	**Tools & Techniques**	**Outputs**
Schedule Management Plan	Precedence Diagramming Method (PDM)	Project Schedule Network Diagrams
Activity List	Dependency Determination	Project Documents Updates
Activity Attributes	Leads and Lags	
Milestone List		
Project Scope Statement		
Enterprise Environmental Factors		
Organizational Process Assets		

Estimate Activity Resources

Inputs	Tools & Techniques	Outputs
Schedule Management Plan	Expert Judgment	Activity Resource Requirements
Activity List	Alternatives Analysis	Resource Breakdown Structure
Activity Attributes	Published Estimating Data	Project Documents Updates
Resource Calendars	Bottom-Up Estimating	
Risk Register	Project Management Software	
Activity Cost Estimates		
Enterprise Environmental Factors		
Organizational Process Assets		

Estimate Activity Durations

Inputs	Tools & Techniques	Outputs
Schedule Management Plan	Expert Judgment	Activity Duration Estimates
Activity List	Analogous Estimating	Project Documents Updates
Activity Attributes	Parametric Estimating	
Activity Resource Requirements	Three-Point Estimate	
Resource Calendars	Group Decision-Making Techniques	
Project Scope Statement	Reserve Analysis	
Risk Register		
Resource Breakdown Structure		
Enterprise Environmental Factors		
Organizational Process Assets		

Develop Schedule		
Inputs	**Tools & Techniques**	**Outputs**
Schedule Management Plan	Schedule Network Analysis	Schedule Baseline
Activity List	Critical Path Method	Project Schedule
Activity Attributes	Critical Chain Method	Schedule Data
Project Schedule Network Diagrams	Resource Optimization Techniques	Project Calendars
Activity Resource Requirements	Modeling Techniques	Project Management Plan Updates
Resource Calendars	Leads and Lags	Project Documents Updates
Activity Duration Estimates	Schedule Compression	
Project Scope Statement	Scheduling Tool	
Risk Register		
Project Staff Assignments		
Resource Breakdown Structure		
Enterprise Environmental Factors		
Organizational Process Assets		

Control Schedule		
Inputs	**Tools & Techniques**	**Outputs**
Project Management Plan	Performance Reviews	Work Performance Information
Project Schedule	Project Management Software	Schedule Forecasts
Work Performance Data	Resource Optimization Techniques	Change Requests
Project Calendars	Modeling Techniques	Project Management Plan Updates
Schedule Data	Leads and Lags	Project Documents Updates
Organizational Process Assets	Schedule Compression	Organization Process Assets Updates
	Scheduling Tool	

Plan Cost Management		
Inputs	**Tools & Techniques**	**Outputs**
Project Management Plan	Expert Judgment	Cost Management Plan
Project Charter	Analytical Techniques	
Enterprise Environmental Factors	Meetings	
Organizational Process Assets		

Estimate Costs		
Inputs	**Tools & Techniques**	**Outputs**
Cost Management Plan	Expert Judgment	Activity Cost Estimates
Human Resource Management Plan	Analogous Estimating	Basis of Estimates
Scope Baseline	Parametric Estimating	Project Document Updates
Project Schedule	Bottom-Up Estimating	
Risk Register	Three-Point Estimate	
Enterprise Environmental Factors	Reserve Analysis	
Organizational Process Assets	Cost of Quality	
	Project Management Software	
	Vendor Bid Analysis	
	Group Decision-Making Techniques	

Determine Budget		
Inputs	**Tools & Techniques**	**Outputs**
Cost Management Plan	Cost Aggregation	Cost Baseline
Scope Baseline	Reserve Analysis	Project Funding Requirements
Activity Cost Estimates	Expert Judgment	Project Document Updates
Basis of Estimates	Historical Relationships	
Project Schedule	Funding Limit Reconciliation	
Resource Calendars		
Risk Register		
Agreements		
Organizational Process Assets		

Control Costs		
Inputs	Tools & Techniques	Outputs
Project Management Plan	Earned Value Management	Work Performance Information
Project Funding Requirements	Forecasting	Cost Forecasts
Work Performance Data	To-complete Performance Index (TCPI)	Change Requests
Organizational Process Assets	Performance Reviews	Project Management Plan Updates
	Project Management Software	Project Documents Updates
	Reserve Analysis	Organization Process Assets Updates

Project Quality Management Knowledge Area

Plan Quality Management		
Inputs	Tools & Techniques	Outputs
Project Management Plan	Cost-Benefit Analysis	Quality Management Plan
Stakeholder Register	Cost of Quality	Process Improvement Plan
Risk Register	Seven Basic Quality Tools	Quality Metrics
Requirements Documentation	Benchmarking	Quality Checklists
Enterprise Environmental Factors	Design of Experiments	Project Documents Updates
Organizational Process Assets	Statistical Sampling	
	Additional Quality Planning Tools	
	Meetings	

Perform Quality Assurance		
Inputs	**Tools & Techniques**	**Outputs**
Quality Management Plan	Quality Management and Control Tools	Change Requests
Process Improvement Plan	Quality Audits	Project Management Plan Updates
Quality Metrics	Process Analysis	Project Documents Updates
Quality Control Measurements		Organization Process Assets Updates
Project Documents		

Control Quality		
Inputs	**Tools & Techniques**	**Outputs**
Project Management Plan	Seven Basic Quality Tools	Quality Control Measurements
Quality Metrics	Statistical Sampling	Validated Changes
Quality Checklists	Inspection	Verified Deliverables
Work Performance Data	Approve Change Requests Review	Work Performance Information
Approved Change Requests		Change Requests
Deliverables		Project Management Plan Updates
Project Documents		Project Documents Updates
Organizational Process Assets		Organization Process Assets Updates

Plan Human Resource Management		
Inputs	**Tools & Techniques**	**Outputs**
Project Management Plan	Organization Charts and Position Descriptions	Human Resource Management Plan
Activity Resource Requirements	Networking	
Enterprise Environmental Factors	Organizational Theory	
Organizational Process Assets	Expert Judgment	
	Meetings	

Acquire Project Team		
Inputs	**Tools & Techniques**	**Outputs**
Human Resource Management Plan	Pre-Assignment	Project Staff Assignments
Enterprise Environmental Factors	Negotiation	Resource Calendars
Organizational Process Assets	Acquisition	Project Management Plan Updates
	Virtual Teams	
	Multi-criteria Decision Analysis	

Develop Project Team		
Inputs	**Tools & Techniques**	**Outputs**
Human Resource Management Plan	Interpersonal Skills	Team Performance Assessments
Project Staff Assignments	Training	Enterprise Environmental Factors Updates
Resource Calendars	Team-building Activities	
	Ground Rules	
	Colocation	
	Recognition and Rewards	
	Personnel Assessment Tools	

Manage Project Team		
Inputs	**Tools & Techniques**	**Outputs**
Human Resource Management Plan	Observation and Conversation	Change Requests
Project Staff Assignments	Project Performance Appraisals	Project Management Plan Updates
Team Performance Assessments	Conflict Management	Project Documents Updates
Issue Log	Interpersonal Skills	Enterprise Environmental Factors Updates
Work Performance Reports		Organization Process Assets Updates
Organizational Process Assets		

Project Communications Management Knowledge Area

Plan Communications Management		
Inputs	**Tools & Techniques**	**Outputs**
Project Management Plan	Communication Requirements Analysis	Communications Management Plan
Stakeholder Register	Communication Technology	Project Documents Updates
Enterprise Environmental Factors	Communication Models	
Organizational Process Assets	Communication Methods	
	Meetings	

Manage Communications		
Inputs	**Tools & Techniques**	**Outputs**
Communications Management Plan	Communication Technology	Project Communications
Work Performance Reports	Communication Models	Project Management Plan Updates
Enterprise Environmental Factors	Communication Methods	Project Documents Updates
Organizational Process Assets	Information Management Systems	Organization Process Assets Updates
	Performance Reporting	

Control Communications		
Inputs	**Tools & Techniques**	**Outputs**
Project Management Plan	Information Management Systems	Work Performance Information
Project Communications	Expert Judgment	Change Requests
Issue Log	Meetings	Project Management Plan Updates
Work Performance Data		Project Documents Updates
Organizational Process Assets		Organization Process Assets Updates

Project Risk Management Knowledge Area

Plan Risk Management		
Inputs	**Tools & Techniques**	**Outputs**
Project Management Plan	Analytical Techniques	Risk Management Plan
Project Charter	Expert Judgment	
Stakeholder Register	Meetings	
Enterprise Environmental Factors		
Organizational Process Assets		

Identify Risks		
Inputs	**Tools & Techniques**	**Outputs**
Risk Management Plan	Documentation Reviews	Risk Register
Cost Management Plan	Information Gathering Techniques	
Schedule Management Plan	Checklist Analysis	
Quality Management Plan	Assumptions Analysis	
Human Resource Management Plan	Diagramming Techniques	
Scope Baseline	SWOT Analysis	
Activity Cost Estimates	Expert Judgment	
Activity Duration Estimates		
Stakeholder Register		
Project Documents		
Procurement Documents		
Enterprise Environmental Factors		
Organizational Process Assets		

Perform Qualitative Risk Analysis		
Inputs	**Tools & Techniques**	**Outputs**
Risk Management Plan	Risk Probability and Impact Assessment	Project Documents Updates
Scope Baseline	Probability and Impact Matrix	
Risk Register	Risk Data Quality Assessment	
Enterprise Environmental Factors	Risk Categorization	
Organizational Process Assets	Risk Urgency Assessment	
	Expert Judgment	

Perform Quantitative Risk Analysis		
Inputs	**Tools & Techniques**	**Outputs**
Risk Management Plan	Data Gathering and Representation Techniques	Project Documents Updates
Cost Management Plan	Quantitative Risk Analysis and Modeling Techniques	
Schedule Management Plan	Expert Judgment	
Risk Register		
Enterprise Environmental Factors		
Organizational Process Assets		

Plan Risk Responses		
Inputs	**Tools & Techniques**	**Outputs**
Risk Management Plan	Strategies for Negative Risks or Threats	Project Management Plan Updates
Risk Register	Strategies for Positive Risks or Opportunities	Project Documents Updates
	Contingent Response Strategies	
	Expert Judgment	

Control Risks		
Inputs	**Tools & Techniques**	**Outputs**
Project Management Plan	Risk Assessment	Work Performance Information
Risk Register	Risk Audits	Change Requests
Work Performance Data	Variance and Trend Analysis	Project Management Plan Updates
Work Performance Reports	Technical Performance Measurement	Project Documents Updates
	Reserve Analysis	Organization Process Assets Updates
	Meetings	

Plan Procurement Management		
Inputs	**Tools & Techniques**	**Outputs**
Project Management Plan	Make-or-Buy Analysis	Procurement Management Plan
Requirements Documentation	Expert Judgment	Procurement Statement of Work
Risk Register	Market Research	Procurement Documents
Activity Resource Requirements	Meetings	Source Selection Criteria
Project Schedule		Make-or-Buy Decisions
Activity Cost Estimates		Change Requests
Stakeholder Register		Project Documents Updates
Enterprise Environmental Factors		
Organizational Process Assets		

Conduct Procurements		
Inputs	**Tools & Techniques**	**Outputs**
Procurement Management Plan	Bidder Conference	Selected Sellers
Procurement Documents	Proposal Evaluation Techniques	Agreements
Source Selection Criteria	Independent Estimates	Resource Calendars
Seller Proposals	Expert Judgment	Change Requests
Project Documents	Advertising	Project Management Plan Updates
Make-or-Buy Decisions	Analytical Techniques	Project Documents Updates
Procurement Statement of Work	Procurement Negotiations	
Organizational Process Assets		

Control Procurements		
Inputs	**Tools & Techniques**	**Outputs**
Project Management Plan	Contract Change Control System	Work Performance Information
Procurement Documents	Procurement Performance Reviews	Change Requests
Agreements	Inspections and Audits	Project Management Plan Updates
Approved Change Requests	Performance Reporting	Project Documents Updates
Work Performance Reports	Payment Systems	Organization Process Assets Updates
Work Performance Data	Claims Administration	
	Records Management System	

Close Procurements		
Inputs	**Tools & Techniques**	**Outputs**
Project Management Plan	Procurement Audits	Closed Procurements
Procurement Documents	Procurement Negotiations	Organization Process Assets Updates
	Records Management System	

Project Stakeholder Management Knowledge Area

Identify Stakeholders		
Inputs	**Tools & Techniques**	**Outputs**
Project Charter	Stakeholder Analysis	Stakeholder Register
Procurement Documents	Expert Judgment	
Enterprise Environmental Factors	Meetings	
Organizational Process Assets		

Plan Stakeholder Management

Inputs	Tools & Techniques	Outputs
Project Management Plan	Expert Judgment	Stakeholder Management Plan
Stakeholder Register	Meetings	Project Documents Updates
Enterprise Environmental Factors	Analytical Techniques	
Organizational Process Assets		

Manage Stakeholder Engagement

Inputs	Tools & Techniques	Outputs
Stakeholder Management Plan	Communication Methods	Issue Log
Communications Management Plan	Interpersonal Skills	Change Requests
Change Log	Management Skills	Project Management Plan Updates
Organizational Process Assets		Project Documents Updates
		Organization Process Assets Updates

Control Stakeholder Engagement

Inputs	Tools & Techniques	Outputs
Project Management Plan	Information Management Systems	Work Performance Information
Issue Log	Expert Judgment	Change Requests
Work Performance Data	Meetings	Project Management Plan Updates
Project Documents		Project Documents Updates
		Organization Process Assets Updates

www.ingramcontent.com/pod-product-compliance
Lightning Source LLC
Chambersburg PA
CBHW050241290326
41930CB00043B/3273